All About the Bundt

Cheryl St.John

Barbara,
Happy baking!
♡♡
Cheryl

ISBN-13: 978-0-9889045-4-5

EAT CAKE!

IT'S SOMEONE'S BIRTHDAY SOMEWHERE

CONTENTS

A big shout out to my beta testers,
who baked, tasted, served and critiqued
several of the cakes in this book.
It was a tough job, but somebody had to do it.

Jodi Allen
Marilyn Bradsby
Judy Esposito
Brenda Mazur
Megan Poe
Robyn Roberts
Carla Snyder
Kimberly Spear
*lizzie starr
Ronnie Swanson
Tami Wirth

Bundt® Pan Facts

A Bundt cake is a cake baked in a special pan, shaping it into a distinctive ring shape with a central tube that leaves a hole in the center of the cake. The shape is inspired by a traditional European cake known as *Gugelhupf*, originally popular among Jewish communities in Germany, Austria and Poland. There is also a Scandinavian version called *kugelhopf*. The design means that more of the mixture touches the surface of the pan than in a simple round pan, helping to provide faster and more even heat distribution during cooking.

The Bundt pan was created in 1950, and in 1966 Ella Helfrich baked a cake called the "Tunnel of Fudge" and took second place at the annual Pillsbury Bake-Off, winning $5,000. The cake was baked in a Bundt pan. The resulting publicity resulted in more than 200,000 requests to Pillsbury for Bundt pans and soon led to the Bundt pan surpassing the tin Jell-O® mold as the most-sold pan in the United States.

- The first Bundt pan was created in 1950 by H. David Dalquist the founder of Nordic Ware located in St. Louis Park, MN.
- Nearly 60 million Bundt pans are in circulation in the world
- Nordic Ware can turn out nearly 30,000 Bundt pans a day.
- The Bundt pan has been seen on the silver screen, with a starring performance in "My Big Fat Greek Wedding".
- There are nearly 50 different Bundt pan shapes in addition to the traditional design.
- In July of 2007, The Bundt pan and other Nordic Ware artifacts were recognized and accepted in the Smithsonian.
- A Bundt pan isn't a true Bundt, if it isn't made by Nordic Ware.
- Bundt pans are American made, produced in Minneapolis, Minnesota.

Bundt® is a registered trademark of Northland Aluminum Products based in Minneapolis, MN and produced under the Nordic Ware brand.

Bundt Cake How-To

- There is a difference between a tube pan and a Bundt pan. A tube pan is more shallow, while a Bundt pan has higher sides. Each will hold a different amount and will bake the same batter differently.

- If you don't own one, buy a flour sifter. My Aunt Marilyn was the best baker ever, and I learned from her to *always* sift flour, whether the package says pre-sifted or not, whether the recipe calls for it or not. Never skip this step. I sift baking soda, baking powder, salt and spices with the flour. If you want to get fanatical, sift your cake mixes as well.

- As you do when making muffins, mix wet and dry ingredients separately, then blend them together on the medium setting of the mixer just before pouring into the pan. Overmixing makes the cake tough.

- When creaming sugar and butter or shortening, have the butter at room temperature, mix on medium and add the sugar gradually.

- Don't overbeat eggs. Mix with a whisk or on low with the mixer, just until blended. For a lighter cake, add eggs one at a time, blending well after each.

- If you use cooking spray, be sure to buy non-stick—the kind with flour in it. Spray just before pouring the batter into the pan—don't let it sit while you prepare the batter, because the spray will run to the bottom. Spray doesn't always cut it though. If in doubt, grease with shortening or butter and dust with flour (or cocoa for chocolate cakes) to help the cake rise in the pan.

- Baking time varies depending on your oven and your pan. I use my convection oven setting. My heavy Nordic Ware® pan bakes more quickly than my silicone pan, so when using it I take off 5-10 minutes baking time and check the cake often.

- After removing it from the oven, cool the cake on a wire rack for ten to fifteen minutes (unless the directions read differently). Any longer and you risk the cake sticking to the pan.

- Don't pack the cup when measuring flour. Dip into flour and scrape off excess with the flat edge of a knife.

How to Use a Silicone Bundt Pan

Specific baking and care tips for silicone pans

Credit: ehow.com

* Preheat the oven to the temperature required in the cake recipe. Silicone is heat resistant up to 500 degrees F. Since this is the highest temperature ovens will reach, you can safely use your silicone Bundt pan in the oven at any temperature.

* Spray the inside of the silicone Bundt pan with cooking spray.

* Place the Bundt pan on top of a baking sheet. This will both prevent the pan from discoloring if your oven is set to a high temperature and give you a stable surface to bake the cake on.

* Pour the cake batter into the cake pan, filling no higher than ¾ of the way full. Use the excess batter in another pan or save it for later use.

* Place the cake pan on top of the baking sheet and then into the oven to bake for the prescribed time.

* Check the cake 5 minutes before the lowest time recommended in the recipe by inserting a dried strand of spaghetti into the center. If the spaghetti comes out cleanly, the cake is ready. Cakes baked in silicone Bundt pans might bake faster or slower depending upon how evenly and quickly your oven heats. You might have to add a few minutes.

* Use oven mitts to remove the cake pan on top of the baking sheet from the oven. Leave the cake pan on the baking sheet until the cake has completely cooled.

* Turn the silicone Bundt pan upside down over the serving platter and gently move the sides and shake the pan until the cake comes out cleanly on the platter.

* Hand wash your silicone Bundt pan in soap and water and let air dry.

Cheryl's Note: I have washed mine in the dishwasher with good results.

About My Recommended Brands

I tested recipes using the brands and products mentioned, but you may certainly substitute whatever you have in your cupboards.

I use nothing but Light Grey Celtic Sea Salt® for table salt, cooking and baking. It's sold in health food stores, and from their website. Learn more at: http://www.celticseasalt.com/

Or you can subscribe and save on amazon.

Celtic Sea Salt® has several times the mineral & moisture content of other leading salt brands. It's doctor recommended, with less sodium, so it's safe for low sodium diets and has many health benefits. I drink ½ teaspoon dissolved in a glass of hot water every morning.

I'm a fan of Ghirardelli cocoas, though my beta testers tried many of the recipes using Hershey. I use only almond milk for drinking, baking and cooking, but beta testers used regular milk with good results.

NO SKILL REQUIRED

Several recipes in this collection are labeled NO SKILL REQUIRED, indicating exceptional ease of preparation. If you don't consider yourself a baker or if you're an accomplished baker and simply want a quick recipe, you will find these cakes using box mixes are convenient and delicious. You don't have to tell anyone you started with a mix—the cakes are so good that no one will guess preparation didn't take hours. Bake with ease and enjoy serving a beautiful cake to family and friends.

I experimented with a lemon cake until I got an extraordinarily lemony and delicious cake that slices easily and looks beautiful. This cake is one of my favorites and always a hit.

Tip: Grate peel from several lemons at once. Measure 3 Tablespoons into each of a few snack bags and freeze so you're always ready to make this cake.

Glazed Citrus Bundt Cake

Preheat oven to 350° | Grease and flour Bundt pan well.

¾ cup softened butter
3 cups sugar
5 eggs, whisked
3 Tablespoons lemon zest (3-4 lemons, depending on size)
1 teaspoons pure vanilla
1 - 2 teaspoons lemon extract
3 cups *sifted* flour
1 cup Sprite or Squirt

Beat butter with electric hand mixer.
Add sugar one cup at a time and mix until creamy.
Add eggs one at a time, mixing briefly after each.
Stir in lemon zest and extracts.
On medium speed, alternate adding flour and Sprite.
Don't overbeat.
Pour batter into prepared pan.

Baking time varies depending on your oven and your pan. I use my convection oven setting. My heavy Nordic Ware® pan bakes more quickly than my silicone pan. In the Nordic Ware® I bake this about 40 - 45 minutes, then cover with foil for another ten. Test and if a toothpick doesn't come out clean, add more time. Remove from oven and cool on a wire rack ten minutes. After ten minutes remove cake from pan and allow to cool.

Citrus Glaze:
2 cups powdered sugar
4 Tablespoons Rose's sweetened lime juice
(I find this in the liquor section)

Lemon Poppy Seed Cake

NO SKILL REQUIRED

¼ cup poppy seeds
¼ cup lemon juice
I box lemon cake mix
1 small package instant vanilla pudding mix
1 cup water
½ cup light olive oil
4 eggs

Preheat oven to 350° | Grease and flour Bundt pan well.

Prior to baking:
Soak poppy seeds in lemon juice for 1 to 2 hours

Whisk dry cake mix and dry pudding mix.
In separate bowl whisk eggs, oil and water.
Blend together with electric mixer on medium speed.
Mix in poppy seeds.
Pour batter into prepared pan.
Bake 45-50 minutes.
(See section on how baking times vary according to pan type.)
Cool pan on rack for 10-15 minutes and turn out onto plate.

Glaze:

1 cup powdered sugar

1-2 Tablespoons water or lemon juice, depending on your preference.

Keep the mixture thick and drizzle over cooled cake.

Triple Chocolate Bundt Cake

NO SKILL REQUIRED

Moist and chocolatey!

Preheat oven to 350° | Grease and flour Bundt pan well.
(or spray and dust with cocoa)

4 eggs
¾ cup sour cream
½ cup oil
½ cup water
1 4-ounce package instant chocolate pudding
1 chocolate cake mix
1 cup semi-sweet chocolate chips

Beat the eggs with a mixer, then add sour cream until blended smooth.
Add oil and water. Mix well.

Whisk dry ingredients and add to liquid mixture, stirring only until combined.
Batter will be thick.

Pour into pan and bake 50-55 minutes or until cake tests done.

No frosting is necessary for this moist cake, but if you want to take it over the top, dust with powdered sugar, or spoon warm cherry pie filling or Cool Whip on individual pieces.

Caramel Bundt Cake

3 cups *sifted* flour
1 ¼ cup sugar
½ tsp baking powder
½ tsp baking soda
½ tsp Celtic Sea Salt®
3 teaspoons real vanilla extract
1 cup sour cream
2 sticks unsalted butter, softened
5 large eggs, room temperature

Preheat oven to 350° | Grease and flour Bundt pan well.

Sift together flour, baking powder, baking soda and salt.
With electric mixer beat butter until creamy.
Add sugar to butter and mix until light.
Add eggs one at a time
Add sour cream until well blended.
Add vanilla.

Combine flour mixture ½ cup at a time until well combined.
Pour into pan.
Bake 50 minutes.
Cool 10-12 minutes before inverting onto a rack.
Make the glaze while the cake cools completely, about an hour.

Caramel Glaze: *(or skip this step and use a jar of ice cream topping)*

1 cup sugar
¾ cup heavy cream
½ stick of butter
Celtic Sea Salt®, coarse ground

Melt butter and sugar over medium heat, stirring constantly.
Add cream and continue to stir until bubbly.
Let cool before drizzling over cake.
Sprinkle coarse Celtic Sea Salt® over the top.

Perfect Caramel Apple Bundt Cake

NO SKILL REQUIRED

1 box yellow cake mix
1 small package instant vanilla pudding
1 cup water
4 eggs, whisked
⅓ cup light olive oil or ½ cup applesauce
3 Granny Smith apples, peeled and chopped
Caramel topping (or 20 caramels, melted with ¼ cup milk)

Preheat oven to 350° | Grease and flour Bundt pan well.

Whisk dry cake mix and dry instant pudding mix.
Add water, eggs and oil and mix on high until well blended.
Stir in apples.

Pour into prepared pan.
Bake 50 minutes or until cake tests done.

Cool 15 minutes in pan and turn out onto wire rack.

After cake is completely cooled, drizzle caramel over the top. Sprinkle lightly with coarse ground Celtic Sea Salt® or kosher salt if desired.

Arbor Day Apple Bundt Cake

Nebraskans celebrate Arbor Day. We visit Arbor Lodge, attend the Applejack Festival and visit the orchards in Nebraska City.

3 cups sifted flour
1 teaspoon baking soda
2 teaspoon cinnamon
½ teaspoon nutmeg
½ teaspoon Celtic Sea Salt®

2 sticks salted butter
1 ½ cups sugar
½ cup light brown sugar
4 eggs, whisked
3 ½ cups chopped tart apples, like Honey Crisp, Pink Lady or Granny Smith
1 cup chopped walnuts
2 teaspoon pure vanilla

Preheat oven to 325° | Grease and flour Bundt pan well.

Sift flour, soda, spices and salt; make a well and set aside. Cream butter and sugars. Add eggs one at a time, beating well after each.
Pour into flour mixture and blend well.
Add apples, nuts and vanilla. Stir.
Pour batter into greased pan. Bake 1 hour 15 minutes.
Cool in pan on rack 15 minutes. Invert onto plate.

Glaze:

3 Tablespoon butter
3 Tablespoons light brown sugar
3 Tablespoons sugar
3 Tablespoons heavy cream
¼ teaspoon pure vanilla

Combine in saucepan and bring to a boil. Boil I minute. Remove from heat and allow to cool. Drizzle over cake.

Make-Ahead Sour Cream Chocolate Bundt

2 sticks unsalted butter
⅓ cup cocoa powder
1 teaspoon Celtic Sea Salt®
1 cup water
2 cups sifted flour
1 ¾ cups sugar
1 ½ teaspoons baking soda
3 large eggs
½ cup sour cream
1 teaspoon vanilla

Preheat oven to 350° | Grease and flour Bundt pan well.

In a small saucepan, combine butter, cocoa, salt, and water. Place over medium heat, stirring, just until melted. Remove from heat and set aside.

Place the flour, sugar, and baking soda in a large bowl and whisk to blend. Add half of the melted butter mixture and whisk until completely blended. (the mixture will be thick) Add the remaining butter mixture and whisk until combined. Add eggs, whisking one at a time until completely blended. Whisk in the sour cream and vanilla until smooth.

Pour batter into prepared pan and bake 40-45 minutes or until a toothpick inserted into the center comes out clean.

Cool on rack 10 minutes and then invert onto the rack. Let cool completely before glazing.

Glaze:

- 4 ounces bittersweet chocolate, finely chopped
- 1 ½ Tablespoons agave nectar or corn syrup
- ½ cup heavy cream
- 1 ½ Tablespoons sugar

Place chopped chocolate and corn syrup in a glass bowl and set aside.

Stir heavy cream and sugar in a small saucepan until the cream is hot and the sugar is dissolved. Pour hot cream over the chocolate and whisk until melted and smooth. Letting it stand a minute or two will allow it to thicken.

Drizzle over cooled cake.

Streusel Bundt Cake

3 cups sifted flour
1 Tablespoon baking powder
½ teaspoon Celtic Sea Salt®
¼ teaspoon baking soda
1 stick butter or margarine
2 cups sugar
4 large eggs
2 teaspoon pure vanilla
8 ounces sour cream
1 cup chopped pecans
½ cup firmly packed light brown sugar
½ cup semi-sweet miniature chocolate chips
2 teaspoons cinnamon

Preheat oven to 350° | Grease and flour Bundt pan well.

Whisk together flour, baking powder, salt and baking soda in a medium bowl; set aside.

Cream butter and sugar with electric mixer until light and fluffy—about 5 minutes.
Whisk eggs and add.
Beat in vanilla, scraping sides.

On low speed, alternately beat in flour mixture and sour cream, starting with flour mixture. Don't overbeat.
Combine pecans, brown sugar, chocolate chips and cinnamon in medium bowl; set aside.

Spoon a third of the cake batter into greased pan.
Sprinkle with half of the pecan mixture.
Spoon half of the remaining batter over pecan mixture; spread to cover. Repeat with remaining pecan mixture and cake batter.

Swirl with knife to marbleize; smooth top.

Bake 55 minutes or until toothpick inserted in center comes out clean.

Cool 10 minutes on rack; remove from pan and cool completely.

Before serving, sift powdered sugar over top.

Mocha
Latte
Chocolate

Pumpkin & Spice & Everything Nice

2 sticks butter or margarine
3 eggs, whisked
1 cup packed brown sugar
1 ¼ cups sugar
1 (15 ounce) can pumpkin puree
3 cups sifted flour
2 teaspoons baking soda
1 teaspoon Celtic Sea Salt®
3 ½ teaspoons cinnamon
1 teaspoon nutmeg
½ teaspoon allspice
½ teaspoon ginger
½ cup chopped pecans, optional

Preheat oven to 350° | Grease and flour Bundt pan well.

Sift together flour, baking soda, salt, cinnamon, nutmeg, allspice, and ginger. Set aside.

Cream butter, eggs, brown sugar and white sugar until light and fluffy.
Beat in the pumpkin puree.
Beat in the flour mixture.
Stir in the chopped pecans.
Pour batter into greased pan.

Bake 55-65 minutes or until a toothpick inserted into the center comes out clean.

Let cool for 10 minutes, then invert on wire rack and cool completely.

Chocolate Almond Cake with Macaroon Filling

1 stick unsalted butter
1 ¾ cups sugar
1 egg yolk
2 teaspoons almond extract
4 eggs
2 cups sifted flour
½ cup unsweetened cocoa
1 teaspoon baking soda
1 teaspoon Celtic Sea Salt®
¾ cup ice water
½ cup sour cream

Macaroon Filling:

1 egg white
¼ cup sugar
1 cup flaked coconut
1 Tablespoon sifted flour
1 teaspoon almond extract

Slivered almonds for topping (how to toast: page 36)

Preheat oven to 350° | Grease and flour Bundt pan well.

Set a small glass bowl in the refrigerator for later.

Cream butter and 1 ¾ cups sugar
Combine egg yolk and almond extract, beat until smooth. Add to sugar mixture.
Beat in eggs one at a time using an electric mixer.
Sift together 2 cups flour, cocoa, baking soda and salt; stir into the egg mixture alternately with the sour cream and water.
Pour batter into greased pan.

Wash beaters, rinse with COLD water. Whip the egg white in the cold bowl until soft peaks form. Gradually sprinkle in 1/4 cup sugar and whip to firm peaks. Fold in the coconut, 1 Tablespoon flour and 1 teaspoon almond extract by hand using a spatula. Drop this mixture by spoonsful over the chocolate batter in the pan. Don't let the filling touch the sides of the pan.

Bake for 55-65 minutes or until a knife inserted comes out clean.

Cool for 10 minutes in the pan, then invert onto rack.
Cool completely.

Glaze:

2 cups sifted confectioner's sugar
1 Tablespoon butter, softened
1 teaspoon almond extract
2 Tablespoons milk

Combine confectioners' sugar, butter and milk, adding milk gradually until thick but pourable. Drizzle over cake. Scatter slivered almonds over the top.

How to toast slivered almonds:

Spread in a single layer on shallow baking dish or cookie sheet.

Bake 5 minutes in 350° oven; remove, shake to rearrange, and return to oven. After an additional 5 minutes, check again. If they are dark enough, remove from oven. If they need more browning, shake again and return to the oven.

Check every couple of minutes to avoid overcooking. Don't roast over 15 minutes.

Share-or-Else Candy Bar Cake

a chocolate lover's dream

10 regular-size Milky Way candy bars
3 sticks margarine, not butter
2 cups sugar
4 eggs, whisked
2 ½ cups sifted flour
1 teaspoon baking soda
1 cup buttermilk
(or add 1 teaspoon white vinegar to one scant cup milk)
2 ½ teaspoons pure vanilla
½ cup chopped nuts, optional
2 cups powdered sugar

Preheat oven to 325° | Grease Bundt pan.
Dust with cocoa powder and tap off excess

Sift flour and baking soda. Set aside.
Melt 7 candy bars with 1 stick of margarine; stir smooth. Set aside.
Cream sugar and 1 stick margarine.
Add eggs, beat until smooth.
Add buttermilk to the flour mixture.
Add melted candy bars, 2 teaspoons vanilla and nuts
Pour batter into prepared pan.
Bake 50-60 minutes at 325 degrees or until cake tests done.

Cool on wire rack 15 minutes before inverting onto plate.
Cool completely.

Icing:
Melt the remaining 3 candy bars and stick of margarine, whisk smooth.
Add ½ teaspoon vanilla and powdered sugar. Pour over cake.

Godiva Mocha Bundt Cake

I won a bottle of Godiva Chocolate Liqueur at the Romance Authors of the Heartland Christmas party, and I put that prize to good use!

¾ cup unsalted butter, softened
2 cups sugar
¾ cup unsweetened cocoa
4 egg yolks
1 teaspoon baking soda

2 Tablespoons cold water
½ cup strong-brewed coffee
1 cup Godiva Chocolate Liqueur®, divided
2 Tablespoons pure vanilla
1 ⅓ cups sifted flour
4 egg whites

Preheat oven to 325° | Grease and flour Bundt pan well.

Separate eggs. Place a deep glass mixing bowl in the refrigerator.

In a large measuring cup dissolve baking soda in water, then add coffee,½ cup of the Godiva Chocolate Liqueur®, and extract.
Cream butter and sugar until light and fluffy.
Beat in cocoa.
Whisk the egg yolks and add.
Alternately beat in flour and coffee mixture until moistened.
Beat egg whites on high in the cold bowl until stiff peaks form.
Fold ⅓ of the whites into the batter, then carefully fold in remaining whites until no streaks remain.
Pour batter into greased pan. Bake 60 minutes or until a toothpick inserted comes out clean.

Cool in pan for 10 minutes, then invert onto a wire rack. Pierce warm cake with a meat fork and drizzle glaze over cake.
Store in container or wrap cake to preserve moisture.

Glaze:
Combine 1 cup powdered sugar and remaining ½ cup of Godiva Chocolate Liqueur®.

Not-To-Be-Forgotten Hummingbird Cake

NO SKILL REQUIRED

I didn't come up with this recipe, but I have tweaked it. This cake has been around since the 1950s. If you look on Pinterest you'll see many versions. It's easy and requires no skill. Cake mix Bundt cakes are a snap.

1 yellow cake mix
1 - 3.4 ounce package vanilla instant pudding and pie filling
½ light olive vegetable oil
1 (8-ounce) can crushed pineapple, drain and reserve juice
4 eggs, whisked
1 teaspoon cinnamon
1 ripe banana, cut up
½ cup finely chopped pecans
¼ cup chopped maraschino cherries, drained
½ cup Betty Crocker Rich and Creamy cream cheese frosting

Preheat oven to 350° | Grease and flour Bundt pan well.

Combine cake and pudding mixes, oil, pineapple, eggs, and cinnamon.
Add enough water to pineapple juice to make 1 cup; add it to the bowl. Beat with mixer until thoroughly combined.

Fold in banana, pecans, and cherries; mix well.
Pour batter into greased pan.

Bake 55-60 minutes or until toothpick inserted in center comes out clean. Let cake cool in pan 20-25 minutes, then invert onto serving plate. Let cool completely.

Measure ½ cup of frosting into glass measuring cup and microwave 10-15 seconds. Stir until smooth and pourable then drizzle over cooled cake. Allow to set before slicing.

Banana Nut Cake

This is a beautiful solid cake that slices well and tastes like banana bread.

yellow cake mix
3 eggs, whisked
1 ⅓ cup virgin olive oil
½ cup yogurt
4 ripe bananas, mashed
1 cup chopped walnuts
½ teaspoon cinnamon
cinnamon and sugar sprinkle for the pan

Preheat oven to 350° | Grease or spray Bundt pan well
Liberally sprinkle prepared pan with cinnamon sugar

Combine eggs, oil, yogurt, cinnamon and mashed bananas.
Add to cake mix and blend well with electric mixer.
Stir in walnuts.

Bake 50 minutes or until cake tests done.

Cool in pan for 10-15 minutes before inverting onto plate.

Weighs-a-Pound Bundt Cake

2 sticks unsalted butter, room temperature
3 cups sugar, divided in 2 ½ and ½ cup portions
6 large eggs, separated and room temperature
1 teaspoon pure vanilla
1 tsp almond extract
1 cup sour cream, room temperature
3 cups sifted CAKE flour
¼ tsp baking soda
1 teaspoon Celtic Sea Salt®

Preheat oven to 325° | Butter and flour Bundt pan well.

Place a narrow deep bowl in the refrigerator.

Sift together dry ingredients.
Cream butter and 2 ½ cups sugar until light.
Beat in eggs yolks one at a time.
Beat in extracts.
Alternate adding flour mixture and sour cream, beginning and ending with flour.
Wash beaters and rinse with COLD water.
In the cold bowl beat egg whites until soft peaks form.
Gradually beat in remaining ½ cup sugar until peaks are stiff.
Fold into batter. Pour batter into prepared pan.

Bake 50-65 minutes until toothpick inserted in center comes out clean.
Cool in pan 10-15 minutes before inverting onto plate.

Moist and Easy Cream Cheese Pound Cake

3 sticks unsalted butter, softened
8 ounces cream cheese, softened
3 cups sugar
6 eggs
3 cups sifted flour
1 teaspoon lemon extract
1 teaspoon pure vanilla

Preheat oven to 325° | Grease and flour Bundt pan well.

Cream butter and cream cheese until smooth.
Add sugar and mix well.
Add eggs, blending after each until batter is fluffy.
Blend in flour.
Add extracts.

Pour batter into prepared pan. Bake 75 minutes or until cake tests done.

Cool in pan on rack for 15 minutes before turning out into plate. Cool completely.

Spiced Chiffon Bundt Cake

2 ½ cups sifted cake flour
1 ½ cups sugar
1 Tablespoon baking powder
1 teaspoon cinnamon
½ teaspoon nutmeg
½ teaspoon allspice
⅛ teaspoon cloves
½ cup extra virgin olive oil
7 egg yolks
¾ cup cold water
7 egg whites, refrigerated in deep glass bowl
½ teaspoon cream of tartar
Icing and ½ cup slivered almonds for garnish

Heat oven to 350° | Do not grease pan.
Will also bake well in an angel food cake pan

Whisk dry ingredients including spices. Make a well.
Add oil, yolks and water and beat until well satin smooth.

Wash beaters. Rinse with cold water and dry well.

Use large deep bowl to beat eggs whites and cream of tartar on high until stiff peaks form and stand straight.

Slowly pour batter over eggs whites. Fold in gently with spatula.
Pour batter into ungreased pan.

Place pan on baking sheet and bake 55-65 minutes or until top springs back when touched.

Invert the pan on a bottle neck and allow cake to cool completely. (My cousin told her me her mom always used wooden clothespins to support the inverted pan.)

When cool, loosen sides with a plastic knife and invert onto plate.

Butter Glaze:

3 Tablespoons butter
2 cups sifted powdered sugar
1 teaspoon vanilla
3-4 Tablespoons milk

Heat butter in saucepan over medium heat until butter turns brown. Remove from heat.
Place sifted powdered sugar in bowl.
Stir in butter, vanilla and milk. Stir until desired consistency.

Perfectly Pecan Coffee Cake

3 cups sifted flour
½ teaspoon Celtic Sea Salt®
3 teaspoons baking powder
1 tsp baking soda
1 cup butter, softened
1 ½ cup sugar
3 eggs, whisked
1 cup sour cream
1 teaspoon pure vanilla

1 cup chopped pecans
1 Tablespoons sugar
1 teaspoon cinnamon

Preheat oven to 325° | Grease and flour Bundt pan well.

Sift flour, baking powder, salt and soda; make a well; set aside.

Cream butter and sugar, add sour cream; add eggs one at a time, beating after each addition.
Pour liquid mixture into flour mixture and combine well.
Add vanilla.

Pour half the batter into greased and floured pan.

Combine pecans, 3 Tablespoons sugar and cinnamon.
Sprinkle half over batter in pan.
Pour remainder of batter over pecan mixture. Spread evenly.
Top with remaining pecan mixture.
Bake 50-55 minutes or until cake tests done.

Cool 10-15 minutes in pan before inverting on cake plate.
Cool completely.

Chocolate Peanut Butter Cake

1 devil's food cake mix
1 cup creamy peanut butter
1 ⅓ cups water
¼ cup light olive oil
½ teaspoon pure vanilla
4 eggs, whisked
½ cup heavy cream

Preheat oven to 350° | Grease and flour Bundt pan well.

Melt peanut butter in large bowl in microwave.
Add oil, water and cream and mix well.
Add eggs and combine well.
Add cake mix and vanilla and blend.
Pour into greased pan.
Bake 45-55 minutes or until toothpick inserted in center comes out clean.

Cool in pan on wire rack 10-15 minutes, then invert to plate.

Frosting:

¾ cup semi-sweet chocolate chips
½ teaspoon pure vanilla
1 Tablespoon unsalted butter

Melt together, stirring well. Pour over cooled cake.
Sprinkle with chunks of topping.

Topping:

6 mini peanut butter cups, chopped
Optional: 1 cup dry-roasted peanuts

Another choice for peanut butter lovers is Easy Peanut Butter Frosting

Pumpkin Bundt Cake

1 yellow cake mix, reserve ¾ cup
1 small can pumpkin pie filling
4 eggs, whisked
¾ cup softened butter
½ cup milk

Reserved ¾ cup cake mix
½ stick softened butter (not melted)
¼ cup sugar
1 teaspoon cinnamon

Preheat oven to 350° | Grease and flour Bundt pan well.

Combine pumpkin, ¾ cup butter, milk and eggs; beat well. Add to cake mix. Pour half the batter into greased pan.

Combine ½ stick soft butter, reserved cake mix, cinnamon and sugar with fork, so it's crumbly.
Sprinkle over batter in pan.
Pour remaining batter over top, spread evenly.
Bake 45-50 minutes.

Cool in pan 10 minutes on rack, then invert onto plate.

Drizzle with Plain Glaze:

¼ cup butter
2 cups powdered sugar
3 Tablespoons water
1 teaspoon pure vanilla

Chocolate Turtle Latté Cake

NO SKILL REQUIRED

1 chocolate cake mix
12 ounce bag semi-sweet chocolate chips
¾ cup chopped pecans plus ¼ cup for top
4 eggs, whisked
½ cup light olive oil
½ cup strong coffee
1 cup sour cream
1 teaspoon pure vanilla
1 large box instant chocolate pudding

Preheat oven to 350° | Grease and flour Bundt pan well.

Combine 2 Tablespoons of cake mix, ¾ cup pecans and chocolate chips.
Stir until coated.

Mix remaining cake mix, eggs, oil, coffee, sour cream, vanilla and pudding on medium until well blended.
Fold in chip and nut mixture.
Pour into prepared pan.
Bake 45-55 minutes until cake tests done.

Cool on rack in pan 15 minutes before inverting onto rack.
Cool completely.

Glaze:

½ cup butter
2 teaspoons milk
½ cup brown sugar
Celtic Sea Salt®, coarse ground

Bring to a boil to melt the brown sugar.

Let cool a little and place waxed paper under the edges of the cake before drizzling. Sprinkle coarse Celtic Sea Salt® over the top.

Garnish with ¼ cup pecans while glaze is still warm. Remove waxed paper once the glaze is set.

Easy Rocky Road Bundt Cake

NO SKILL REQUIRED

1 chocolate cake mix
1 small box instant chocolate pudding mix
1 cup sour cream
3 eggs, whisked
½ cup plus 2 Tablespoons mini semisweet chocolate chips, divided
½ cup plus 2 Tablespoons chopped walnuts, divided
2 cups marshmallow creme

Preheat oven to 350° | Grease and flour Bundt pan well.

Prepare cake batter according to package directions, using 3 eggs.
Add instant pudding mix and sour cream. Blend well.
Stir in ½ cup chocolate chips and ½ cup walnuts.
Pour into prepared pan.

Bake 40 to 50 minutes or until toothpick inserted in center comes out clean.

Cool in pan on wire rack 15 minutes.
Invert cake onto wire rack to cool completely.
Move to cake plate when cooled.

Topping:
Melt marshmallow creme in microwave 15 seconds or more.
Spray a spatula with nonstick cooking spray before stirring.
While still hot, pour over cake.
Immediately top with remaining 2 Tablespoons of chocolate chips and 2 Tablespoons walnuts.

Store cake loosely covered, not in an airtight container.

Rocky Road Bundt Cake

1 ¼ cups water
¾ cup Ghirardelli unsweetened cocoa powder

2 ¼ cups sugar
1 teaspoon Celtic Sea Salt®
2 ½ teaspoons baking soda
3 eggs
1 ¼ cups buttermilk
1 cup light olive or canola oil
1 ½ teaspoons pure vanilla
1 teaspoon almond extract (optional)
2 ¾ cups sifted flour
1 cup toasted sliced almonds
1 cup mini chocolate chips

Marshmallow Glaze:

1 ½ cups confectioners' sugar
1 teaspoon pure vanilla
¼ teaspoon Celtic Sea Salt®
4 Tablespoons unsalted butter
2 cups mini-marshmallows

Preheat oven to 350°
Grease Bundt pan; dust with cocoa powder and tap out excess. Refrigerate pan until ready to use.

Reserve 2 Tablespoons each of sliced almonds and mini-chocolate chips. Set aside for topping.

How to toast slivered almonds:
Spread in a single layer on shallow baking dish or cookie sheet.
Bake 5 minutes in 350° oven; remove, shake to rearrange, and return to oven. After an additional 5 minutes, check again. If they are dark enough, remove from oven. If they need more browning, shake again and return to the oven. Check every couple of minutes to avoid overcooking. Don't roast over 15 minutes.

Whisk water and cocoa powder in a small saucepan and bring to a boil over medium heat, whisking frequently. Remove from heat and let come to room temperature.

Whisk sugar, salt and baking soda.
Cream together with eggs.
Blend in buttermilk, oil, vanilla and almond extract.
Slowly add flour and blend well.
Add the cooled cocoa mixture and mix well.
Pour batter into prepared pan and bake for 55-65, or until a toothpick inserted in the cake comes out clean.

Let the cake cool completely in the pan and then invert onto a cooling rack.

Glaze:
Combine sugar, vanilla, and salt in a bowl.
Melt the butter along with 2 Tablespoons of water over medium-high heat. Remove from heat and immediately add marshmallows and stir until completely melted.
Whisk into sugar mixture until smooth.
Drizzle over cake.
Sprinkle with toasted almonds and chocolate chips.

Coke® Bundt Cake

1 box devil's food cake mix
1 cup Coca-Cola®
½ cup buttermilk (no substitutions)
8 Tablespoons unsalted butter, melted
3 large eggs, whisked
1 cup mini marshmallows

Preheat oven to 350°
Grease Bundt pan; dust with cocoa powder and tap out excess.

Mix together butter and eggs. Add buttermilk and Coke®.
Blend in cake mix; mix until smooth.
Fold in marshmallows.
Pour batter into the prepared pan.
Bake 40-45 minutes, or until inserted toothpick comes out clean.

Let cake cool in the pan for 5-10 minutes before inverting onto plate.
Cool completely.

Frosting:

4 Tablespoons butter
½ cup Coke®
½ teaspoon almond extract
½ cup semi-sweet chocolate chips
4 cups powdered sugar

Melt butter, cola and almond extract and whisk while bringing to a simmer. Turn off heat, add chocolate chips, and stir until melted.
Pour into a bowl and add powdered sugar one cup at a time, mixing on medium speed until smooth. Pour over cake.

Old-Fashioned Cocoa Bundt Cake

¾ cup softened butter or margarine
1 ⅔ cups sugar
3 eggs, whisked
2 cups sifted flour
⅔ cups Ghirardelli unsweetened cocoa powder
1 ¼ teaspoon baking soda
½ teaspoon baking powder
1 teaspoon Celtic Sea Salt®
1 ⅓ cups milk
1 teaspoon pure vanilla
½ teaspoon peppermint extract
⅓ cup crushed peppermint candies for garnish

Preheat oven to 350° | Grease and flour Bundt pan well.

Whisk together flour, soda, baking powder and salt.
Make a well and set aside.
In another bowl cream butter and sugar.
Add eggs one at a time and beat 3 minutes on high.
Alternately add egg mixture and milk to flour mixture.
Add vanilla. Blend in crushed candies.

Bake 35-45 minutes. Cool in pan on rack 10 minutes.
Turn out on cake plate. Cool completely.

Peppermint Fudge Frosting

(or use Chocolate Dream Frosting)

½ cup butter or margarine
½ cup Ghirardelli unsweetened cocoa powder
1 lb. (3 ⅔ cups) powdered sugar
7 Tablespoons milk
½ teaspoon pure vanilla
½ teaspoon peppermint extract

Melt butter, add cocoa and whisk until smooth.
Alternately add powdered sugar and milk.
Beat until well blended.
Blend in vanilla; add candies. Cool and pour over cake.
Garnish.

Chocolate Zucchini Bundt Cake

2 cups sifted flour
½ teaspoon Celtic Sea Salt®
1 ½ teaspoon baking soda
⅓ cup Ghirardelli unsweetened cocoa powder
1 cup sugar
1/3 cup light olive oil
3 eggs, whisked
1 teaspoon pure vanilla
¾ cup sour cream
3 cups grated zucchini, drained on a towel or paper towels
1 cup semi-sweet mini-chocolate chips
1 cup Craisins®

Soak Craisins® in ¾ cup water.
Preheat oven to 350° | Grease and flour Bundt pan well.

Whisk flour, salt, soda, and cocoa. Make a well; set aside.
Cream oil and sugar. Add eggs and vanilla. Beat well.
Add sour cream and mix until blended.
Drain Craisins®. Add Craisins® and chocolate chips; stir in.
Pour batter into prepared pan.
Bake about 45 minutes or until toothpick inserted in center comes out clean.

Cool 10 minutes in pan before inverting on rack. Cool completely.

Molasses Spice Bundt Cake

1 cup butter, softened
1 cup sugar
6 eggs, separated
1 cup molasses
2 cups sifted flour
1 teaspoon Celtic Sea Salt®
1 teaspoon allspice
1 teaspoon cinnamon
1 teaspoon cloves
1 teaspoon nutmeg
8 ounces sour cream
1 teaspoon baking soda
powdered sugar

Preheat oven to 300° | Grease and flour Bundt pan well.

Whisk flour, salt and spices. Make a well and set aside.
Cream butter and sugar until light and fluffy.
Add egg yolks and molasses beat well.
Beginning and ending with flour mixture, alternately add flour mixture and sour cream.
Beat room temperature eggs whites until stiff peaks form; gently fold into batter. Pour batter into prepared pan.

Bake 1 hour and 40 minutes or until cake tests done.

Cool in pan 10 minutes; remove from pan and cool completely.

Frost or sift powdered sugar over top.

Oreo® Cookie Bundt Cake

NO SKILL REQUIRED

1 white cake mix
1 ¼ cups water
½ cup light olive oil
3 eggs, whisked
2 cups coarsely crushed Oreo® Cookies

Preheat oven to 350° | Grease and flour Bundt pan well.

Combine all ingredients, except crushed cookies at medium speed 2 minutes.
Fold in crushed cookies with spatula.
Pour batter into prepared pan.
Bake 30-40 minutes or until cake tests done.

Cool 10-15 minutes in pan on wire rack before inverting onto plate.

Frost or glaze. Choices in the section *Frostings*

Fudge Pudding Cake

NO SKILLS REQUIRED

Sometimes I discover a great recipe just by using what's on hand. That's how I came up with this moist and chocolatey Bundt cake. It's best on the second day, after standing covered. It slices beautifully.

Preheat oven to 350°
Spray Bundt pan well just before adding batter.

Super Moist German chocolate cake mix
1 large box chocolate pudding, not instant
¾ cup mayonnaise
½ cup oil
3 eggs, whisked

Combine mayonnaise, oil and eggs. Add cake mix and pudding mix.
Mix on high until batter is smooth and creamy.
Pour batter into sprayed pan
Bake 50 minutes until cake tests done.

Cool on rack 14 minutes. Invert onto plate.

Topping options:

Heat ¾ cup canned frosting and drizzle over cake.
Spoon cherries over top.
Top with whipped cream.
Serve with strawberry Jell-o®

Chocolate Raspberry Bundt Cake

NO SKILL REQUIRED

1 devil's food cake mix
½ cup water
⅓ cup light olive oil
3 eggs, whisked
1 cup seedless raspberry jam

2 cups fresh or frozen raspberries

Preheat oven to 350° | Grease and flour Bundt pan well.

Combine cake mix, water, oil and eggs on medium for 2 minutes.
Stir in jam and mix well.
Pour batter into prepared pan and bake 30 minutes or until cake tests done.

Cool in pan on wire rack for 10 minutes, then invert onto plate.

Serve slices with whipped cream and fresh raspberries.

French Silk Bundt Cake

2 sticks softened butter
7 ounce jar marshmallow creme
3 ounces unsweetened chocolate, chopped
5 eggs, whisked
1 cup heavy cream
½ cup strong-brewed coffee
2 ½ cups sifted flour

Preheat oven to 350° | Grease Bundt pan well
Dust with cocoa powder and tap out extra

Heat butter, marshmallow crème and chocolate in heavy saucepan, whisking until chocolate is melted and mixture is smooth. Set aside.

Whisk together eggs, heavy cream and coffee.
Add flour and chocolate alternately ton egg mixture, starting with flour, mixing until batter is smooth. Don't overbeat.
Pour into prepared pan and bake 50 minutes or until cake tests done.

Cool in pan in wire rack 10-15 minutes before inverting onto plate. Cool completely.

Frost with French Silk Frosting or Marshmallow Creme Frosting.

Shave chocolate on top for garnish if desired.

French Silk Frosting:

2 ⅔ cups powdered sugar
⅔ cup softened butter
2 squares melted unsweetened chocolate, cooled
¾ teaspoon pure vanilla
2 Tablespoons heavy cream

With electric mixer. Cream butter and sugar until smooth. Add chocolate. Add vanilla on low speed. Add cream, beat until silky.

Buttermilk Bundt with Caramel Frosting

2 sticks softened butter
2 ½ cups sugar
5 eggs, whisked
2 teaspoons pure vanilla
3 cups sifted flour
1 Tablespoon baking powder
1 ½ teaspoons Celtic Sea Salt®
1 cup buttermilk (no substitutes)

Preheat oven to 350° | Grease and flour Bundt pan well

Whisk flour with baking powder and salt. Make a well and set aside.
Beat butter with electric hand mixer.
Add sugar one cup at a time and mix until creamy.
Add eggs one at a time, mixing briefly after each.
Stir in vanilla.
On medium speed, alternate adding flour and buttermilk.
Don't overbeat.
Pour batter into prepared pan.
Bake 45-55 minutes or until cake tests done.

Cool in pan on wire rack 15 minutes before inverting onto plate. Cool completely.

Real Caramel Frosting:

2 cups sugar
1 cup buttermilk
1 cup butter
1 teaspoon baking soda

Combine ingredients in heavy saucepan and whisk constantly to soft ball stage 235° – 245° or when a small amount dropped in cold water forms a ball. Remove from stove; cool and beat until spreadable.

Sour Cream Chocolate Cake

¾ cup boiling water
6 ounces semisweet chocolate chips
¾ cup Ghirardelli unsweetened cocoa powder
1 ¾ cups sifted flour
1 teaspoon Celtic Sea Salt®
1 teaspoon baking soda
5 eggs, room temperature, whisked
2 cups packed light brown sugar
1 ½ sticks unsalted butter, melted
1 teaspoon pure vanilla
1 cup sour cream

Preheat oven to 350° | Grease and flour Bundt pan well.

Combine flour, soda, salt and set aside.

Cream eggs, brown sugar and vanilla until smooth and creamy.
Stir chocolate chips into boiling water and stir over low heat until melted.
Add cocoa and whisk until smooth.
Add egg and sugar mixture to flour mixture and combine well.
Add sour cream. Mix well.
Add chocolate mixture. Beat until smooth and creamy.
Pour batter into prepared pan.
Bake 50-60 minutes or until cake tests done.

Cool in pan on write rack 10 minutes; turn out onto wire rack and cool.

Dust with powdered sugar.

Devil's Food Bundt Cake

Sift together:
2 cups flour
½ cup Ghirardelli unsweetened cocoa powder
1 ½ teaspoons baking powder
½ teaspoon Celtic Sea Salt®

Whisk together:
3 large eggs
¾ cup buttermilk
1 cup packed dark brown sugar
1 cup applesauce
¾ cup dark corn syrup
2 teaspoons pure vanilla

Preheat oven to 350°
Grease and sift cocoa powder into Bundt pan.
Tap out excess.

Whisk dry ingredients in large bowl and make a well.

Whisk liquid ingredients and pour half at a time into the dry mixture and blend until smooth, two or three minutes on medium speed.
Pour into prepared pan.
Bake 30-40 minutes or until a toothpick inserted comes out clean.

Cool cake in pan on wire rack for 10 minutes before inverting onto rack.

Egg White Frosting:

2 large egg whites
pinch of salt
1 ½ cups sugar
⅓ cup water
2 teaspoons vanilla or other extract

Combine ingredients in glass bowl and whisk.
Microwave 30-45 seconds until hot (don't boil), whisk at intervals to dissolve sugar.
Remove from microwave and beat on medium until it cools some and whips up. When you like the consistency for spreading it's done.

Chocolate Bundt Cake

1 ½ cups strong-brewed coffee
¾ cup Ghirardelli unsweetened cocoa powder
2 ¼ cups sugar
1 ¼ teaspoons Celtic Sea Salt®
2 ½ teaspoons baking soda
2 large eggs
1 egg yolk
1 cup buttermilk
1 cup light olive oil
2 teaspoon pure vanilla
2 ½ cups sifted flour

Preheat oven to 350°
Grease and sift cocoa powder into Bundt pan.
Tap out excess.

Bring cocoa powder and coffee to a boil, whisking constantly.
Remove from heat and allow to cool.

Cream sugar, salt, baking soda, eggs, and yolk.
Beat on low 1 minute.
Add buttermilk, oil, and vanilla and beat until smooth.
Add flour to sugar and egg mixture and beat well until smooth.
Add cooled cocoa/coffee mixture and beat until smooth.
Pour batter into pan and bake for about 50-60 minutes or until a toothpick inserted in center comes out clean.

Cool cake in pan on a wire rack for 20-30 minutes before inverting onto plate.

Real Chocolate Frosting:

6 ounces unsweetened chocolate squares
¾ cup unsalted butter
3 cups powdered sugar
½ cup sour cream, at room temperature
¼ cup strong-brewed coffee, cooled
¼ cup half and half or cream

Chop the chocolate into pieces and melt with butter in the microwave.
Stir often while it's melting. Whisk smooth.
Add half the powdered sugar and whisk again. The mixture will be thick.
Whisk in sour cream and remaining powdered sugar.
Add coffee and cream and whisk together until glossy.
Add cream until frosting reaches the preferred consistency.

Walnut Date Bundt Cake

16 ounces chopped pitted dates
1 ½ cups boiling water
1 ½ teaspoons baking soda
2 ¼ cups all-purpose flour
1 ½ teaspoons baking powder
¼ teaspoon Celtic Sea Salt®
1 cup unsalted butter, softened
½ cup brown sugar, packed
3 large eggs
1 ½ teaspoons pure vanilla
1 teaspoon orange zest
1 ½ cups chopped walnuts

Preheat oven to 350° | Grease and spray Bundt pan well.

Pour boiling water over chopped dates and allow to stand a few minutes. Stir in baking soda.

Whisk flour, baking powder and Celtic Sea Salt
Cream butter and brown sugar until smooth.
Add eggs to sugar mixture one at a time, beating well after each addition. Beat in vanilla and orange zest.

Add flour mixture in 1 cup increments just until combined.
Stir in the date mixture and walnuts.
Pour batter into prepared Bundt pan.
Bake 50-55 minutes or until cake tests done.

Cool in pan on wire rack 10-15 minutes before inverting onto plate.
Allow to cool completely.

Glaze:

1 cup powdered sugar
2 Tablespoons orange juice
1 Tablespoon orange zest

Pistachio Swirl Bundt Cake

NO SKILLS REQUIRED

1 box yellow cake mix
1 small box pistachio instant pudding mix
4 eggs, whisked
1 cup water
½ cup light olive oil
½ cup Hershey's chocolate syrup

Preheat oven to 350° | Spray Bundt pan well.

Combine cake mix, pudding mix, eggs, water and oil until smooth.

Remove 1 cup of batter and place in a small bowl.
Add ½ cup chocolate syrup to the 1 cup of batter.
Stir until the chocolate color is uniform.

Pour yellow cake batter into prepared pan.
Pour chocolate syrup mixture over yellow.
Using a plastic knife, swirl gently. Don't overmix.
Bake 45-55 minutes until a toothpick inserted in center comes out clean.

Cool in pan 10-15 minutes before inverting cake onto a plate.

Black Forest Cherry Cake

I got this recipe from a friend many, many years ago, and she got it from her mom. It can't be improved upon, and it never fails to please. It's been my favorite cake since the first time I made it.

Black Forest Cherry Cake

NO SKILL REQUIRED

Preheat oven to 350° | Grease and spray Bundt pan well.

1 package chocolate cake mix
¼ cup light olive oil
3 eggs
2 cans cherry pie filling
Cool Whip for topping, if desired

Combine all except I can of cherries; beat well with mixer until batter is smooth. Pour into greased pan and bake 45 minutes (40 minutes for a Nordic Ware® pan).

Cool in pan 15-20 minutes, then invert onto plate to cool. Serve warm with the other can of cherries spooned over the top.

Store any leftovers in a container in the fridge.

Chocolate Rhubarb Cake

Chocolate Rhubarb Cake

MINIMUM SKILL REQUIRED

Prepare ahead:

6-8 cups chopped rhubarb
2 cups sugar
¼ cup water

Please in heavy saucepan and bring to boil. Turn down heat; simmer and stir, while mixture bubbles about 20 minutes or until foamy. Cool, cover and refrigerate.

Preheat oven to 350° | Grease and spray Bundt pan well.

1 package chocolate cake mix
¼ cup light olive oil
3 eggs
2 cups cook rhubarb

Combine first three ingredients; beat well with mixer until batter is smooth.

Add 2 cups rhubarb sauce, reserving remainder of rhubarb for topping.

Pour into greased pan and bake about 40 minutes (40 minutes for a Nordic Ware® pan).

Cool in pan 20 minutes, then invert onto plate to cool. Warm the remaining rhubarb sauce and spoon over slices to serve.

Don't-Judge-Me Cake

NO SKILLS REQUIRED

yellow cake mix
¼ cup light brown sugar
¼ cup granulated sugar
1 box instant vanilla pudding mix
2 teaspoons cinnamon
4 eggs, whisked
¾ cup water
¾ cup extra virgin olive oil
½ cup white wine

Preheat oven to 350° | Grease and spray Bundt pan well.

Use hand mixer to combine sugars, eggs, oil, water and wine.
Add cake mix, cinnamon and pudding mix and beat until smooth, but don't overbeat.

Bake 60 minutes until cake tests done. Immediate pour glaze over cake while still in pan.

Overkill Glaze:
    1 stick melted butter
    1 cup granulated sugar
    ¼ cup white wine

Heat butter, sugar and wine until combined and dissolved. Pour over hot cake.

Cool cake completely on wire rack.
When cool, turn out onto plate.

Orange Chocolate Bundt Cake

3 ½ cups cake flour
1 Tablespoon baking powder
¾ teaspoon baking soda
1 teaspoon Celtic Sea Salt®
2 sticks (1/2 pound) unsalted butter, room temperature
2 cups sugar
4 large eggs, room temperature
2 teaspoons pure vanilla
2 cups sour cream
½ teaspoon orange extract
zest of 1 large orange
4 Tablespoons Ghirardelli unsweetened cocoa powder
½ cup chocolate chips

Preheat oven to 350° | Grease and flour Bundt pan well.

Sift together flour, baking powder, baking soda and salt and set aside.
Cream butter and sugar at medium speed until pale.
Add eggs one at a time, beating well after each.
Beat in vanilla.
Reduce speed to low, alternately add flour mixture and sour cream until smoothly blended.
Divide batter into two bowls.
In one bowl add orange zest and orange extract. Mix well.
In the other bowl add sifted cocoa powder and chocolate chips. Mix well.
Pour orange batter into the prepared pan, spreading evenly.
Add the chocolate batter on top of the orange. Don't marbleize.

Bake 45 minutes - 1 hour or until a toothpick pick inserted in center comes out clean.

Remove from oven and cool in pan 20-30 minutes.
Invert onto a cooling rack and cool completely.

Peach Dream Cake

2 sticks softened salted butter
3 cups sugar
6 eggs, room temperature
1 teaspoon pure vanilla
3 cups sifted flour
¼ teaspoon baking soda
½ teaspoon salt
½ cup sour cream
2 cups chopped peaches
(4-6 peaches)

Preheat oven to 350°
Spray a Bundt pan well.

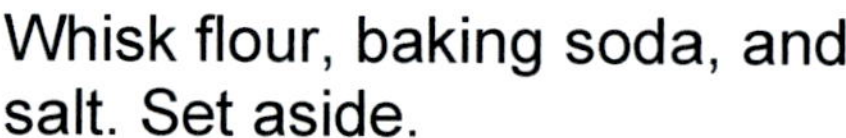

Whisk flour, baking soda, and salt. Set aside.
Cream butter and sugar until light and fluffy.
Add eggs one at a time, beating well after each.
Stir in vanilla.
Stir flour mixture into egg mixture.
Add sour cream and beat on low until smooth.
Fold in peaches.
Pour batter into prepared pan.

Bake 60-65 minutes or until a toothpick inserted in center comes out clean.
See tips on baking times for different types of pans.

Cool in pan on wire rack for 15 minutes before inverting onto plate.

Dust with powdered sugar when cool or use Plain Frosting Glaze.

Strawberry Delight Bundt Cake

NO SKILLS REQUIRED

1 package white cake mix
1 cup sour cream
¼ cup water
2 eggs
1 small box strawberry-flavored gelatin

Preheat oven to 350° | Spray a Bundt pan well.

Beat all ingredients except gelatin for 2 minutes until smooth.
Pour one-third of batter into pan.
Sprinkle evenly with half of the dry gelatin.

Repeat layers with batter and gelatin, then top with remaining batter.
Bake 45-50 minutes or until a wooden toothpick inserted in center comes out clean.

Cool in pan on wire rack 10-15 minutes before inverting onto plate.

Serve with sliced strawberries and whipped topping.

Snickerdoodle Bundt Cake

I'll be honest. I'm not a snickerdoodle fan. But I'm a realist, so I know a lot of people do, so for all the Snickerdoodle fans, here's your cake!

Combine:

2 teaspoons ground cinnamon
1 cup sugar

2 ½ cups sifted flour
1 teaspoon baking powder
½ teaspoon baking soda
½ teaspoon Celtic Sea Salt
1 cup salted butter, softened
1 cup sugar
1 cup light brown sugar
3 eggs, room temperature
2 teaspoon pure vanilla
1 cup sour cream

Preheat oven to 325° | Spray Bundt pan well.

Mix 1 cup of sugar and 2 teaspoons of cinnamon.
Dust the inside of the pan with about 1/3 cup of the cinnamon and sugar mixture. Set the rest aside.

Sift together flour, baking powder, baking soda and salt. Set aside.

Cream the butter by itself. Add 1 cup sugar and combine until light.
Add brown sugar. Mix until light brown and smooth.
Add the eggs one at a time, beating after each addition.
Stir in the vanilla.
Add the flour mixture alternately with the sour cream; beat well.

Spread half of batter into prepared pan.

Sprinkle with half of remaining cinnamon sugar mixture.
Spread remainder of the batter on.
Sprinkle remaining sugar mixture on top.

Bake 55 to 65 minutes, or until cake tests done.

Cool in pan 10-15 minutes before inverting on plate.

Easy Carrot Cake

NO SKILLS REQUIRED

1 package carrot-cake cake mix
2 small boxes of instant vanilla pudding
½ cup of light olive oil
1 ¼ cups water
4 eggs, whisked
1 cup chopped pecans
1 cup raisins, soaked and drained

Preheat oven to 350° | Spray a Bundt pan well.

Whisk cake mix, and pudding.
Add oil, water and eggs with electric mixer.
Stir in pecans and drained raisins.
Pour into pan and bake 40-45 minutes or until toothpick inserted comes out clean.

Cool in pan on wire rack 10-15 minutes before inverting onto plate.
Cool completely

Frosting:

4 cups powdered sugar
1 8-ounce package cream cheese, softened
3-4 Tablespoons almond milk
1 Tablespoon pure vanilla

Beat cream cheese with powdered sugar and milk until creamy. Stir in vanilla. Spread over cooled cake.

Carrot Cake for Company

1 ½ cups extra virgin olive oil
2 cups sugar
4 eggs, room temperature, separated
5 Tablespoons hot water
2 ½ cups sifted flour
1 ½ teaspoons baking powder
½ teaspoon baking soda
½ teaspoon Celtic Sea Salt®
1 teaspoon cinnamon
1 teaspoon ground cloves
½ teaspoon nutmeg
1 ¾ cups grated raw carrots
1 cup 100% bran cereal
1 /2 cup chopped pecans
powdered sugar for sifting over top

Preheat oven to 350° | Grease and flour Bundt pan well.

On low speed, blend oil and sugar. Add egg yolks one at a time, beating after each. Beat in hot water.

In separate bowl combine flour, baking powder, soda, salt and spices, gradually add to oil & sugar mixture, beating the whole time. Stir in carrots, bran cereal and pecans.

In small bowl beat egg whites until stiff peaks form; fold into batter.

Pour into prepared pan. Bake 60-70 minutes or until cake tests done. Cool in pan 15 minutes on wire rack before inverting. Cool and sift powdered sugar over top before serving or frost with Cream Cheese Frosting on page 96.

Blueberry Zest Bundt Cake

2 sticks softened unsalted butter
2 cups sugar
3 large eggs, whisked
1 Tablespoon pure vanilla
2 teaspoons lemon extract
2 ¾ cups sifted flour
2 teaspoons baking powder
½ teaspoon baking soda
½ teaspoon Celtic Sea Salt
1 ¼ cup buttermilk
1 pint of fresh blueberries, well dried

Preheat oven to 350° | Spray a Bundt pan well.
Mix ¼ cup sugar with ! Tablespoon lemonade mix or ½ teaspoon cinnamon and dust the entire inside of the sprayed pan. Tap off extra.

Whisk flour, baking powder, salt, baking soda. Set aside.
Cream butter and sugar until light and fluffy.
Add eggs one at a time, mixing after each.
Add vanilla and buttermilk. Blend well.
Add egg and sugar mixture to flour mixture and blend only until combined.
Don't overmix.
Very gently stir in half of the blueberries.
Pour batter into pan.
Drop the remaining blueberries on top.

Bake 60-75 minutes or until cake tests done.

Cool completely on wire rack before inverting onto plate.

For the Holidays

Cranberry Bundt

3 cups sifted flour
2 cups sugar
1 teaspoon ground cardamom
1 ½ teaspoons baking powder
½ teaspoon baking soda
1 cup milk
¾ cup melted butter
3 eggs, whisked
1 cup fresh cranberries

Preheat oven to 350° | Grease and flour Bundt pan well.

Whisk dry ingredients in a large bowl and set aside.
Beat butter and eggs on medium speed; add milk.
Combine wet and dry ingredients on medium for 2 minutes.
Stir in cranberries.

Pour into prepared pan.
Bake 50-60 minutes or until cake tests done.

Cool 10-15 minutes before inverting.
Sift powdered sugar over top.

Chocolate Mint Holiday Cake

3 ounce pkg. cream cheese, softened
2 Tablespoons sugar
2 eggs, separated
⅛ teaspoon peppermint extract
3 drops green or red food coloring
1 box devil's food cake mix
1 ⅓ cups water
⅓ cup light olive or canola oil
2 eggs, whisked

Preheat oven to 350° | Grease and flour Bundt pan well.

In a small bowl beat cream cheese on high until fluffy.
Beat in sugar, egg yolks, ⅛ tsp extract and 3 drops food coloring until smooth. Set aside.

Combine cake mix, 1⅓ cups water, oil, 2 eggs plus 2 egg whites on low speed and then beat on high for 2 minutes.

Pour half the batter into prepared pan.
Spoon cream cheese mixture into the center of the batter, not letting it touch the sides of pan.
Spoon remaining batter over top.
Bake 45-50 minutes until toothpick inserted comes out clean.
Cool 45 minutes in pan, then invert onto wire rack and cool.

Frosting:

1 cup powdered sugar
1 teaspoon light olive or canola oil
¼ teaspoon peppermint extract
3 drops green or red food coloring
1 Tablespoon corn syrup
2 – 2 ½ teaspoon water
¼ cup semi-sweet chocolate chips

Whisk until glaze is thick and drizzle over cake.
Immediately sprinkle with chocolate chips.

Applesauce Ginger-Spice Cake

2 ¼ cups sifted flour
1 teaspoon baking soda
½ teaspoon Celtic Sea Salt®
1 ½ teaspoon cinnamon
½ teaspoon allspice
½ teaspoon ground nutmeg
¾ cup chopped pecans
⅓ cup butter, room temperature
1 teaspoon grated lemon zest
⅓ cup light olive or canola oil
¾ cup sugar
⅔ cup light brown sugar
2 large eggs, whisked
1 medium sized Granny Smith apple, peeled and diced (about 1 cup)
1 teaspoon pure vanilla
1 cup applesauce

Preheat oven to 350° | Grease and flour Bundt pan well.

Sift flour, soda, salt and spices. Stir in pecans. Set aside.

Cream butter and shortening a medium speed in large bowl. Add lemon zest, beat until smooth.

Add sugar, a Tablespoon at a time. Blend well.
Add light brown sugar and blend again.
Add eggs, one at a time until blended.
Reduce speed. Add diced apple and vanilla.

Alternate adding flour mixture and applesauce, starting and ending with the flour. Beat only until incorporated.

Pour into prepared pan. Bake 35-40 minutes or cake tests done. Cool in pan 15 minutes before inverting. Glaze with Brown Sugar Glaze on page 96 and garnish with pecans.

Fudge Brownie Cake

1 pkg. chocolate cake mix
1 pkg. fudge brownie mix
4 eggs, whisked
1 ¼ cups water
1 cup extra virgin olive oil
1 can chocolate fudge frosting

Preheat oven to 350° | Grease and flour Bundt pan well.

Combine cake mix, brownie mix, oil, eggs and water until smooth. Pour into prepared pan.

Bake 50-55 minutes or until toothpick inserted comes out clean.

Cool in pan 10 minutes on wire rack cooling rack and then invert. Cool completely before transferring to plate.

Warm half the icing in a small glass measuring pitcher 30 seconds in the microwave and drizzle over cake.

Flavorful Anise Cake

2 ½ cups sifted flour
2 ½ tsp baking powder
½ tsp Celtic Sea Salt®
¾ cup unsalted butter
1 ¾ cup sugar
3 eggs, room temperature
1 ½ teaspoon pure vanilla
1 ¼ cups cream or half and half
1 Tablespoon plus 1 teaspoon anise extract

Preheat oven to 350° | Grease and flour Bundt pan well.
Or, instead of flour, sprinkle with fine breadcrumbs.

Sift flour, baking powder and salt together. Set aside.
Beat butter until creamy.
Slowly add sugar and beat on medium speed 2 minutes.
Add eggs one at a time, beating after each addition.
Add vanilla and anise extract.

Alternate adding flour mixture and milk until all ingredients are combined. Pour batter into prepared pan.

Bake 45 minutes or until cake tests done.

Cool in pan on wire rack 15 minutes before turning out onto serving plate. Cool completely.

Glaze:

¼ cup butter
2 cups powdered sugar
3 Tablespoons water
1 teaspoon anise extract

Cream together ingredients and drizzle over Bundt cake.

Kahlua Cake

NO SKILLS REQUIRED

1 pkg. chocolate fudge cake mix with pudding in the mix
2 eggs, whisked
½ cup Kahlua
¼ cup extra virgin olive oil
16 ounces sour cream
12 ounce pkg. chocolate chips

Preheat oven to 350° | Grease Bundt pan well.
Dust with cocoa and shake off excess.

Beat together all ingredients, except chocolate chips, until smooth. Stir in chocolate chips.

Pour into prepared pan.

Bake 40-50 minutes.

Cool in pan 10-15 minutes before inverting onto plate.

Cool completely and dust with powdered sugar.

Pineapple Upside Down Bundt

MINIMUM SKILLS REQUIRED

1 stick butter
1 cup firmly packed brown sugar
1 - 20 ounce can pineapple slices, drained
6-8 maraschino cherries
1 pkg. pineapple or yellow cake mix
1 small pkg. instant vanilla pudding
4 large eggs, whisked
1 cup water
½ cup extra virgin olive oil

Preheat oven to 350° | Grease and flour Bundt pan well.

Melt butter in microwave. Add brown sugar and combine well. Pour into bottom of prepared Bundt pan.

Arrange pineapple slices in the brown sugar mixture, pressing them into it. Place a maraschino cherry in the center of each.

Combine cake mix, pudding mix, eggs, water and oil. Beat well with an electric mixer until smooth. Carefully pour batter over the brown sugar mixture and pineapple rings.

Bake 1 hour or until a toothpick inserted in the center comes out clean.

Cool in the pan anywhere from 45 min to 1 hour, giving brown sugar/butter mixture time to set. (Nordic Ware® takes longer to cool.)

Invert onto plate.

Gingerbread Bundt Cake

2 ½ cups sifted flour
1 cup sugar
¼ cup unsweetened cocoa
2 teaspoons ginger
1 ½ teaspoons baking powder
¾ teaspoon baking soda
½ teaspoon Celtic Sea Salt®
½ teaspoon cinnamon
½ teaspoon nutmeg
½ teaspoon cloves
2 eggs, whisked
1 cup molasses
⅔ cup extra virgin olive oil
1 cup water

Preheat oven to 350° | Grease and flour Bundt pan well.

Sift together flour, sugar, cocoa, ginger, baking powder, baking soda, salt, cinnamon, nutmeg and cloves; mix well.

Add molasses and oil to eggs; beat well.
Stir in water.

Add egg mixture to flour mixture; beat just until combined.
Pour batter into prepared pan.

Bake 50-55 minutes or until toothpick inserted in center comes out clean.

Cool in pan on wire rack for 15 minutes.
Invert cake onto serving plate.
Cool completely.
Dust with powdered sugar.

Pumpkin Bundt Cake
NO SKILLS REQUIRED

1 box yellow or white cake mix
½ cup sugar
½ cup olive oil
1 – 15 ounce can pumpkin
¼ cup water
1 teaspoon cinnamon
1 teaspoon allspice
4 eggs, whisked

Preheat oven to 350° | Grease and flour Bundt pan.

Cream sugar, oil, eggs and pumpkin. Add water.
Beat in cake mix, and cinnamon, combine until smooth.

Pour batter into prepared pan.
Bake for 40-50 minutes or until cake tests done.

Cool 15 minutes in pan on wire rack before inverting onto a cake plate. Cool completely.

Glaze:

- 4 Tablespoons butter
- 1 cup powdered sugar
- 2 Tablespoons milk or cream
- ½ teaspoon vanilla

Melt butter in saucepan over low heat and simmer until brown. Pour into bowl and whisk in powdered sugar, milk, and vanilla until smooth.

Drizzle over cake.

Sweet Potato Cake

1 ⅓ cups sugar
1 cup mashed sweet potatoes
⅓ cup shortening
⅓ cup water
1 egg, whisked
1 ⅔ cups sifted flour
1 teaspoon Celtic Sea Salt®
1 teaspoon cinnamon
1 teaspoon baking soda
¼ teaspoon baking powder
¼ teaspoon ginger
⅔ cup raisins, optional
⅓ cup chopped pecans

Preheat oven to 350° | Grease and flour Bundt pan well.

Sift dry ingredients; set aside.
Beat sugar, sweet potatoes, shortening, water and egg.
Add flour mixture to potatoes and mix well.
Stir in raisins and pecans.

Pour into prepared pan.
Bake 45-50 minutes or until cake tests done.

Cool 10 minutes in pan on wire rack before inverting.
Cool completely.

Icing:

¼ cup butter at room temperature
½ - 7 oz. jar marshmallow creme
½ cup powdered sugar
½ teaspoon vanilla

Beat butter and powdered sugar until fluffy.
Stir in fluff and vanilla and mix. Spread.
If you want it thinner to drizzle, warm the butter first.

Eggnog Bundt Cake

½ cup butter
1 cup sugar
2 eggs, room temperature
½ teaspoon vanilla
2 cups sifted flour
4 teaspoons baking powder
½ teaspoon cinnamon
pinch of nutmeg
1 cup eggnog
optional: Craisins® or chopped nuts

Preheat oven to 350° | Grease and flour Bundt pan well.

Sift flour, baking powder, cinnamon and nutmeg, set aside.
Cream butter and sugar.
Add eggs, one at a time, beating after each
Add vanilla and mix.
Alternately add flour mixture and eggnog until smooth.
Pour into prepared pan.

Bake 45 minutes, or until cake tests done.
Cool in pan on rack 15 minutes before inverting onto plate.

Glaze:

1 cup powdered sugar
¼ cup eggnog
¼ teaspoon cinnamon
¼ teaspoon vanilla

Whisk ingredients until smooth and drizzle over cooled cake.

Frostings & Glazes

Butter Glaze

3 Tablespoons butter
2 cups sifted powdered sugar
1 teaspoon vanilla
3-4 Tablespoons milk

Heat butter in saucepan over medium heat until butter turns brown. Remove from heat.
Place sifted powdered sugar in bowl.
Stir in butter, vanilla and milk. Stir until desired consistency.

Chocolate Butter-Silk Frosting

¾ cup sugar
¼ cup sifted flour
3 Tablespoons Ghirardelli unsweetened cocoa
1 cup almond milk
2 stick salted butter
1 Tablespoon extract
1 cup bittersweet Ghirardelli chocolate chips, melted and cooled

In saucepan whisk sugar, flour and cocoa until combined. Add milk and whisk smooth. Lumps will smooth out as the frosting cooks.
Turn heat to medium and cook, stirring until mixture thickens and boils.
Reduce heat to low, cook 2 minutes, stirring constantly.
Remove from heat.
Cool 30-40 minutes until spreadable.

Chocolate Dream Frosting

3 cups powdered sugar
¾ cup Ghirardelli unsweetened cocoa
1 stick salted butter, softened
4 Tablespoons heavy cream
1 teaspoon extract

Sift sugar and cocoa together.
In separate bowl combine 1 cup of the sugar mixture with butter and 1 Tablespoon cream; beat until smooth. Continue in small increments until all ingredients are combined and frosting is smooth and fluffy.
Beat in extract.
Frost cake.

Ghirardelli Chocolate Frosting

¾ cup salted butter, melted
1 cup Ghirardelli unsweetened cocoa powder
4 cups sifted powdered sugar
½ cup almond milk
1 teaspoon almond extract or 1 ½ teaspoon pure vanilla

Beat butter and cocoa.
Alternately add powdered sugar and milk until smooth.
Stir in vanilla.
Cool slightly and drizzle over Bundt cake.

Plain Frosting Glaze

¼ cup butter
2 cups powdered sugar
3 Tablespoons water
1 teaspoon pure vanilla

Cream together ingredients and drizzle over Bundt cake.

Citrus Glaze

2 cups powdered sugar
2 Tablespoons Rose's sweetened lime juice
(I find this in the liquor section)

Chocolate Cream Cheese Frosting

2 cups sifted powdered sugar
¼ cup Ghirardelli unsweetened cocoa powder
8 ounces cream cheese, softened
2 tablespoons butter, softened

Sift powdered sugar and cocoa together.
In a separate bowl cream butter and cream cheese until light.
On low, gradually beat in sugar mixture incrase speed and beat a full minute.
Frost cake.

Real Chocolate Frosting

6 ounces unsweetened chocolate squares
¾ cup unsalted butter
3 cups powdered sugar
½ cup sour cream, at room temperature
¼ cup strong-brewed coffee, cooled
¼ cup half and half or cream

Chop the chocolate into pieces and melt with butter in the microwave.
Stir often while it's melting. Whisk smooth.
Add half the powdered sugar and whisk again. The mixture will be thick.
Whisk in sour cream and remaining powdered sugar.
Add coffee and cream and whisk together until glossy.
Add cream until frosting reaches the preferred consistency.

Egg White Frosting

2 large egg whites
Pinch of salt
1 ½ cups sugar
⅓ cup water
2 teaspoons vanilla or other extract

Combine ingredients in glass bowl and whisk.
Microwave 30-45 seconds until hot (don't boil), whisk at intervals to dissolve sugar.
Remove from microwave and beat on medium until it cools some and whips up. When you like the consistency for spreading it's done.

Chocolate Buttercream Frosting

2 Tablespoons softened butter
¾ cup Ghirardelli unsweetened cocoa powder
2 ⅔ cups powdered sugar
⅓ cup milk or almond milk
1 teaspoon pure vanilla

Cream butter with mixer.
Add cocoa and powdered sugar alternately with milk.
Beat to spreading consistency. Add another Tablespoon of milk if needed.
Blend in vanilla.

Mega Peanut Butter Frosting

3 ounce package softened cream cheese
½ cup creamy peanut butter
2 Tablespoons milk
½ teaspoon vanilla
2 ¼ cups powdered sugar

Beat cream cheese and peanut butter into a thick mixture.
Slowly beat in milk and vanilla.
Add powdered sugar a little at a time until spreading consistency.
Add more if needed.

Suggestion: Top with chocolate morsels after frosting.

Easy Peanut Butter Frosting

3 cups powdered sugar
1/3 cup peanut butter
1 ½ teaspoons vanilla

Cream peanut butter and vanilla. Slowly add powdered sugar until well blended. Heat a few seconds for easier spreading or drizzle.

Chocolate Peanut Butter Frosting

3 Tablespoons softened butter
2 Tablespoons creamy peanut butter
1 teaspoons pure vanilla
1 ¼ cups powdered sugar
2 Tablespoons cocoa
pinch of Celtic Sea Salt®
2 - 3 Tablespoons milk

Cream butter and peanut butter. Add vanilla. Beat in powdered sugar and salt, then add enough milk to spread or drizzle.

Real Caramel Frosting

2 cups sugar
1 cup buttermilk
1 cup butter
1 teaspoon baking soda

Combine ingredients in heavy saucepan and whisk constantly to soft ball stage 235° – 245° or when a small amount dropped in cold water forms a ball. Remove from stove; cool and beat until spreadable.

Real Buttermilk Frosting

1 cup sugar
1 ½ teaspoons baking soda
½ cup buttermilk (no substitutes)
½ cup butter or margarine
1 Tablespoon light corn syrup
1 teaspoon pure vanilla

Combine ingredients in heavy saucepan and whisk constantly to soft ball stage 235° – 245° or when a small amount dropped in cold water forms a ball. Remove from stove; cool and beat until spreadable.

French Silk Frosting

2 ⅔ cups powdered sugar
⅔ cup softened butter
2 sounded melted unsweetened chocolate, cooled
¾ teaspoon pure vanilla
2 Tablespoons heavy cream

With electric mixer. Cream butter and sugar until smooth. Add chocolate. Add vanilla on low speed. Add cream, beat until silky.

Cream Cheese Frosting

4 cups powdered sugar
1 8-ounce package cream cheese, softened
3-4 Tablespoons milk
1 Tablespoon pure vanilla

Beat cream cheese with powdered sugar and milk until creamy. Stir in vanilla. Spread over cooled cake.

Brown Sugar Glaze

3 Tablespoons butter
3 Tablespoons brown sugar, packed
3 Tablespoons heavy cream
¾ cup sifted powdered sugar
½ teaspoon pure vanilla

Melt butter and brown sugar in saucepan. Stir in cream and cook slowly until mixture comes to a low boil. Simmer 1-2 minutes.

Remove from heat and add powdered sugar gradually, whisking until smooth. Add vanilla and whisk.

Add a few drops of cream if needed.
Drizzle immediately. Sets up fast.

About The Baker

Cheryl is the author of more than fifty books--both historical and contemporary romances and a non-fiction book on writing. Her stories have earned numerous awards and are published in over a dozen languages. One thing all reviewers and readers agree on regarding Cheryl's work is the degree of emotion and believability.

In describing her stories of second chances and redemption, readers and reviewers use words like, "emotional punch, hometown feel, core values, believable characters and real life situations." Amazon and Goodreads reviews show her popularity with readers.

When she's not writing fiction, Cheryl enjoys her family, decorating, going to the movies, browsing flea markets and baking. All About The Bundt is her first cookbook.

Cheryl loves hearing from readers.
Send email to SaintJohn@aol.com
Visit Cheryl on the web
From the Heart Blog
Facebook
Twitter
Goodreads
Pinterest

Thank you for your purchase of *All About the Bundt.*

Reviews help a book be seen by more people.

Please consider leaving a review.

Notes

Notes

Notes

Notes

Notes

Notes

Bundt Bloopers

30610654R00066

Made in the USA
San Bernardino, CA
18 February 2016